BIODIVERSITY

BIODIVERSITY

by Dorothy Hinshaw Patent
Photographs by William Muñoz

Clarion Books
NEW YORK

Acknowledgments

The author and photographer want to thank the many parks, refuges, and zoos that provided opportunities for the photographs in this book. In addition, we wish to thank Roland Redmond and Dan Perlman for their help with the manuscript and the photos, as well as Michael Bleyman of the Carnivore Preservation Trust, for his inspiring conversation and his dedication to diversity.

Clarion Books
a Houghton Mifflin Company imprint
215 Park Avenue South, New York, NY 10003
Text copyright © 1996 by Dorothy Hinshaw Patent
Illustrations copyright © 1996 by William Muñoz

The text was set in 13.25-point New Baskerville.
Book design by Carol Goldenberg.

www.houghtonmifflinbooks.com

Manufactured in China.

Library of Congress Cataloging-in-Publication Data

Patent, Dorothy Hinshaw.
Biodiversity / by Dorothy Hinshaw Patent ; photographs by William Muñoz.
p. cm.
Summary: Provides a global perspective on environmental issues while
demonstrating the concept which encompasses the many forms of life on
earth and their interdependence on one another for survival.
ISBN 0-395-68704-7   PA ISBN 0-618-31514-4
1. Biological diversity—Juvenile literature. 2. Biological diversity conservation—
Juvenile literature. 3. Biological diversity—North America—Juvenile
literature. 4. Biological diversity conservation—North America—Juvenile
literature. 5. Biological diversity—Costa Rica—Juvenile literature.
6. Biological diversity conservation—Costa Rica—Juvenile literature.
[1. Biological diversity. 2. Biological diversity conservation.]
I. Muñoz, William, ill. II. Title
QH541.15.B56P38 1996
333.95'16—dc20   95-49982
CIP   AC

SCP 10 9 8 7 6 5 4 3

FOR E. O. WILSON
*who has been an inspiration to me
for more than thirty years.*
—D.H.P.

FOR CHARLES
*Thank you for sharing the knowledge of
unity in diversity so many years ago.*
—W.A.M.

Contents

Introduction

The subject of biodiversity is huge, as large as the millions of species of living things on planet Earth. Finding a way of limiting the topic to the size of a small book was not easy. After much thought, I decided to focus most of the discussion on two parts of the world—North America and Costa Rica, for a number of reasons.

First of all, these two areas contrast dramatically with each other. Most of North America has a temperate climate—warm in summer, cold in winter. Costa Rica is in the tropics—the seasons are defined by rainfall rather than temperature. North America is a huge area, with many species that range widely across its expanse, as well as others that have limited habitats. Costa Rica is one of the world's smallest countries, yet is home to an incredible variety of life, including many species that are very limited in distribution.

Another reason for dealing largely with North America is that most readers of this book live there. So much of what is written about threats to the natural world today concentrate on faraway places. Yet so many of our own native plants, animals, and other living things are in danger of disappearing if we aren't willing to make the effort to save them. Only in the last few years have we made serious efforts to catalog the diversity of life in the United States, and some of the results are amazing. In just one valley of the Glacier National Park area in Montana, for example, scientists have already found twelve hundred different species of beetles, leading researchers to believe there are probably actually three thousand, in just that one small area. Costa Rica has been a world leader in cataloging and protecting biodiversity—we in North America can learn a great deal from this tiny developing nation. As a matter of fact, the Glacier study utilized a technique developed in Costa Rica, of training a nonscientist (called a parataxonomist) in beetle identification and then employing that person to carry out the field work.

Finally, North America and Costa Rica are places of which I have personal knowledge, and a writer communicates best what she has experienced herself. I've lived in the United States all my life and have traveled extensively in both the United States and Canada. I can picture the places in North America I write about, and I love this beautiful continent. I have also been fortunate enough to visit Costa Rica twice and to explore a number of its amazingly various ecosystems, from the dry tropical forests of the northwest through the cloud forest that tops the Continental Divide and down into the eastern slope rain forests, all the way to the torrid eastern coastal rain forests. I have visited the headquarters of the Costa Rican National Biodiversity Institute (INBio) and several research stations where biodiversity is studied.

The subject of biodiversity can be grasped best through specific examples. Once readers understand the basic principles, they can extrapolate them to situations in other areas of the planet. I hope that, through reading this book, people will come to understand the importance of preserving the fabulous diversity of life on Earth, for the sake of the planet and ourselves.

BIODIVERSITY

Cloud forests contain an incredible variety of life. *Photo by Dorothy H. Patent*

CHAPTER ONE

The Miracle of Diversity

I walk slowly up the path along the ridgeline. At this altitude the air is thin and my breath comes hard. I'm atop the Continental Divide in Costa Rica. On one side, all water flows toward the Atlantic Ocean and on the other, it ends up in the Pacific. As a breeze clears the misty air for a moment, I follow a sign pointing to an overlook. I gaze through the thick greenery outward and downward toward the Pacific Ocean. Up here is bright green forest. But in the distance, brown pastures mark the lowlands. Dark green trees trace the courses of rivers that snake down the slopes and through the fields into the sea. Among the farmlands, scattered patches of dry forest, the native trees leafless during this dry season, have somehow survived the chain saw and plow. Up here, the mist keeps living surfaces almost constantly moist. Obtaining water is not a serious problem for the plants and animals in the forest that surrounds me. But down there, life must be able to survive months of searing dry heat, unrelieved by rainfall.

A little farther along the path, a sign points to the left—an overlook toward the Caribbean Sea on the Atlantic side. The mountains of Central America, where the land is narrow, provide the only place on Earth where you can see both the Pacific and Atlantic oceans within a few yards' distance. The view toward the Atlantic is dramatic—a few miles below, the active volcano called Arenal rises up next to a silvery lake, the mountain's top hidden by a cloud of steam. Were it not for the mist

Clouds obscure the distant view from the Continental Divide, looking toward the Atlantic Ocean. *Photo by Dorothy H. Patent*

rising from the lush rain forest stretching down the slopes below, the Caribbean would be just visible in the far distance. The rain forest covering the hills and valleys on the Atlantic side thrives on abundant rainfall—nine feet or more each year, spread out so that each month provides enough water to maintain life easily.

Varieties of Life

From this special place I can see a greater number of habitats—kinds of environments in which living things can be found—than just about anywhere else on Earth. Surrounding me is the high cloud forest, while below, on the Atlantic side, stretches a continuum of different rain forest environments, from high altitude (with cool nights) all the way down to the steamy Atlantic rain forest, where the temperatures vary little from day to night. On the Pacific side, there are rain forests, moist forests, and dry forests, as well as the grassland habitats created by ranchers who cleared away the trees. Rivers, with their own assortments of living things, wend their way through all of these environments. And on both sides I can see oceans, below the surfaces of which

The Pacific side of Costa Rica is drier than the Atlantic side, with
farm fields covering the mountainsides where once there were forests.
The Pacific Ocean is visible far in the distance. *Photo by Dorothy H.
Patent*

The desert is a very harsh environment for living things.

live countless species of plants, animals, and microscopic life. Such variety and richness is almost more than a person can grasp at one time. And this is just one small spot on the surface of the planet.

Life has an amazing ability to adapt to different environments. It can develop mechanisms for surviving extreme heat or cold, wetness or drought, high mountain altitude or deep ocean depths. Each habitat, or set of environmental circumstances, is home to a different assortment of living things that have developed ways of living there successfully.

But traits that favor survival in one kind of environment can prohibit existence in another. A frog with a moist skin that soaks up water from the damp rain forest atmosphere would die after a few minutes in a hot, dry desert. Desert cactuses, on the other hand, are especially adapted to survive in extreme dryness. They grow slowly and conserve water by having thick stems and no leaves so they can endure whatever the desert has to offer. They would be overwhelmed in the rain forest. The rapid growth of young tropical trees and vines would quickly overshadow them and they would die from lack of sunlight.

The combination of life's ability to adapt to different environments and the fact that adaptation to one environment often leads to an inability to survive under different conditions has led to the evolution of millions of life forms. Over the approximately 3.8 billion years since life began, life has changed and evolved more variations than we will ever know. Most of these no longer exist—the dazzling diversity we see today represents only about one percent of all the species that have lived on Earth at one time or another.

From bees and flowers to fish and underwater plants—the variety of life on Earth seems endless.

What Is Biodiversity?

Much of biological science—the study of living things—focuses on the unifying aspects of living systems. All life shares one origin, and some processes of life are the same or very similar in everything alive. The underpinnings of life are the same or similar, even in very different living things. The list of similarities is long: all living things are made up of subunits called cells; cells pass on their traits to the next generation through a code carried by a chemical called DNA (*deoxyribonucleic acid*); cells in everything from bacteria to human beings break down sugars to obtain energy in essentially the same way; and so forth.

Throughout the history of biological science, however, scientists have also noticed differences. While sugar may be broken down similarly by all living things, the special proteins, called enzymes, that carry out the steps in the process may have varying structures from one species to the next. And while DNA carries the genetic code universally, it transmits differences as well as similarities between individuals to the next generation.

Thousands of scientists devote their careers to studying differences among living things at all levels, from genetics and cell biology to the ways in which life adapts to its external environment. Pine trees and maple trees, dogs and cats, fish and birds, tulips and roses are unlike in many ways. Not only do birds look different from fish, birds themselves are diverse. The variations on the theme of "bird" are astounding.

The variety of living things, thriving in almost every earthly environment, is referred to as biodiversity. "Bio" means "life," and "diversity," of course, refers to the differences that life can exhibit. Biodiversity focuses on these differences rather than on the similarities favored by many other branches of science. Biodiversity is a huge idea—it can be approached at any level, from the chemistry of DNA to the variations within one species to the classification of species themselves. It also includes how living things interact with one another and with their physical environment.

Ostriches, owls, and egrets—all are birds, but each has its own unique way of life.

The Florida panther, a unique subspecies of cougar, has been reduced to only a few individuals. Most of the diversity within the subspecies has been lost.

African elephants are endangered because of loss of habitat over much of their former range. *Photo by Lex Salisbury*

Species of organisms sharing a habitat are collectively called a community. The community, plus all the aspects of the physical environment such as water, climate, and soil composition, is called an ecosystem. Communities and ecosystems are very important—important because if we do not understand how organisms interact, we can deprive species of what they need for survival and send them on the road to extinction.

Extinction brings about the loss of biodiversity. Once a species is extinct, its unique traits and its unique ways of interacting with the rest of the world disappear along with it. But the extinction of species is only the most obvious kind of biodiversity loss. When a species is reduced to a few survivors, most of the diversity within that species is gone. And when a forest is clear-cut or a marsh is filled in to create farmland, whole communities of living things disappear. The designation of the study and preservation of biodiversity as a special branch of science (often referred to as "conservation biology") is quite new, even though scientists have studied aspects of biodiversity for hundreds of years.

The concept of biodiversity and its importance to the health of the planet came into focus largely because of the threats to biodiversity that exist in the modern world. In the last fifty years, species that once thrived, such as leopard frogs and tigers, have become threatened with extinction. The list of extinct and endangered species around the world keeps getting longer and longer, almost exclusively because of the activities of our own destructive species.

Why Should We Care?

What difference should it make to us if the diversity of life around the world is diminishing at a growing rate? After all, extinction has been a part of nature ever since life on Earth began. But this wave of destruction is fundamentally different. While humans have brought about extinctions in previous centuries when they spread to new regions, this time our exploding populations and awesome technology are destroying life at a rate far exceeding what has come before. And in earlier times, when people killed off the last specimen of a dying breed, they were probably not aware of what they were doing. Now we do know, we are aware, and we need to accept our responsibility.

We now know that our planet functions as a whole, as if the Earth itself were a living thing, and we know that our destructive activities in one part of the planet not only bring about local extinctions but also affect the whole world, including the welfare of our own species. During 1987 and 1988, burning of the Amazon forests released hundreds of millions of tons of pollutants into the air, including huge quantities of carbon dioxide, a major cause of the greenhouse effect—the warming of the Earth's atmosphere. Not only was the smoke so thick that airports were shut down and people were sent to the hospital—but also much of the pollution reached the upper atmosphere, where it can affect the entire planet. In North America, pollution from power plants in the United States has drifted across the border into Canada, causing acid rain that has killed the life in many lakes and ponds and is also suspected of killing the sugar maple trees many people depend on for a living. The list could go on and on.

As we destroy the natural world in which we live, we do so without knowing the full consequences. We make the dangerous assumption that the problems we create are fixable. Through our ignorance, we could set in motion changes that make the planet uninhabitable. We are playing Russian roulette with our very survival and the survival of our descendants.

Scientists have been studying life for centuries, yet we still know very little about it, especially about the diversity of life on Earth and how it interconnects. For example, scientists recently have learned how important soil fungi are to the health of the forest. Since they live underground and were difficult to study, no one paid much attention to their ecological role. But the fungi—seen by most of us only when they reproduce through mushrooms—feed essential nutrients to the roots of

Modern technology—such as that associated with pumping, transporting, and refining oil—has created many problems for the natural world.

trees and other plants. The fungus filaments are extremely thin—a thimbleful of soil may contain several miles of filaments. We now know that almost every root of every plant receives nutrients from these fungi, called "mycorrhizae." Without them, plants would have a difficult time obtaining enough nutrients to survive. We have no way of knowing what other vital interactions occur in nature that are yet to be discovered.

Harvard biologist E. O. Wilson and other scientists recently attempted to estimate how many species exist on the planet. About 1.4 million species are known, but that figure must represent only a fraction of the actual number of existing species on Earth. Estimates of the real total run all the way from five million to eighty million! How could this be so, after so many years of devoted study? The number of species is enormous, and much of the diversity exists among the smaller organisms on the planet, especially insects and microscopic forms of life that are difficult to collect and identify. In addition, the places of greatest diversity—coral reefs, deep ocean habitats, and tropical rain forests—are the least studied regions on Earth, so scientists are forced to make very rough estimates of the variety of life. Within the last twenty years, new species even of large animals, such as birds and monkeys, have been discovered living deep within the forests.

Destroying what we don't even know exists seems foolish, not only because of our scientific curiosity, but also because of the practical consequences of the losses. About a third of our medicines were originally discovered in plants, some of these only recently. The Pacific yew tree is a scraggly resident of the Pacific Northwest forests, which cloaked the coastal mountain ranges until recent decades. Clear-cut logging of these forests has created a biological desert where once there was beauty and variety, including the Pacific yew as well as the spotted owl and other now endangered species. But the Pacific yew turns out to be

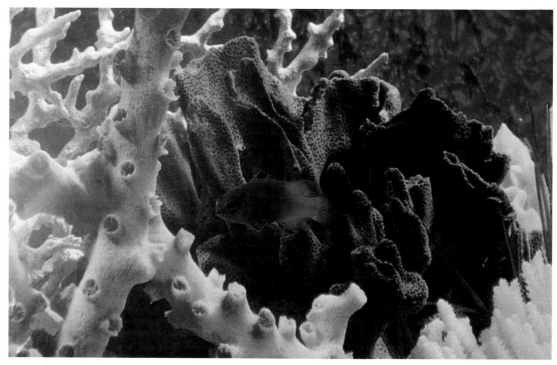

Coral reefs host a great diversity of species.

the source of a treatment for ovarian cancer. Until the discovery of the yew's healing qualities, a diagnosis of ovarian cancer was often a death sentence. There was no effective treatment beyond surgery, and diagnosis of this disease often comes too late for surgery to help. Scientists now know how to manufacture this valuable drug in the laboratory. But if the Pacific yew had drifted into the silent death of extinction, we never would have known of this hopeful treatment.

The island of Madagascar, off the eastern coast of Africa, is a gold mine of biological diversity. Yet most of its forests have already been cleared for agriculture, and many of its unique species have already become extinct. One species that fortunately survived is the rosy periwinkle. This modest pink blossom is the source of two drugs used to treat terrible cancers that usually strike children and that, before the periwinkle came into the picture, were usually fatal. Not only are children given new life by these drugs, the world economy gains an income of

Fortunately, parks such as Glacier National Park protect some of America's western forests.

Much of the world's tropical rain forests remains unexplored. *Photo by Dorothy H. Patent*

around $180 million a year. Five other periwinkles live on Madagascar and could well be sources of other valuable drugs. One of these is already close to extinction because of destruction of its habitat.

In addition to providing medicines, the rain forests could prove to be sources for fast-growing timber species, useful fibers, tasty foods, substitutes for petroleum products, and who knows what other useful products we can't even imagine now.

Practical considerations are not the only reasons for stemming the tide of manmade extinction. Our species evolved in this world, along with all other forms of life. We are part of the living world, and it is part of us. Nature provides us with much more than food, clothing, materials for building, energy sources, medicines, and water. Even residents of highrise apartments in big cities grow flowers on their balconies and houseplants indoors and keep dogs and cats as pets. We depend on other living things and the natural world from which they come for much of our feeling of meaningfulness in life, for a vital part of our emotional and spiritual well-being.

CHAPTER TWO

Adapting to the Environment

Every year I look forward to the autumn, when the leaves on the trees lining the streets of my home town turn yellow, then drop to the ground, forming a golden blanket. I know where to drive to see a flame red maple tree and whose yard has the most brilliant burning bush plants. In my part of the country, the native trees are almost all evergreens—pines, cedars, and spruces, all adapted to a relatively dry, cold climate. Just one of them—the larch—turns amber gold in the fall, then sprinkles its needles lightly onto the land like yellow rain. Those street-lining trees are all imports from moister climates which need more water to survive here than nature provides.

Habitats and Homes

A major reason for the great diversity of life on Earth is the tremendous variety of environments available for life to populate. Through the long process of evolution, each species has developed adaptations that enable it to survive best in a particular combination of climate, terrain, and other living things. This is its favored area, the place where the species is most at home, its habitat.

The number of habitats on Earth, each able to sustain a variety of different species, is enormous. By one count, there are at least thirty-four major habitats in the lower forty-eight states of the United States

From lush, wet ponds to dry shortgrass prairie—North America is home to hundreds of different habitats.

alone. Each of these can be subdivided further. For example, the plains grasslands can be divided into short-grass prairie, tall-grass prairie, and mixed prairie. Some plants and animals inhabit all three prairie types, while others are restricted to one or two types. Scientists who study biodiversity use a long list of habitat types, with four to five hundred for the United States.

Specialists and Generalists

Some species are able to live in a number of different places as long as their basic needs are met. The gray wolf is the most widely distributed mammal in the world other than our own species. It once lived all across the northern hemisphere and southward into the tropic zone in the Arabian Peninsula, India, and Southeast Asia. All wolves need for survival is a supply of prey animals such as caribou or deer, a source of

The gray wolf is a highly successful, widespread species that has been eliminated from much of its historic range.

water, a protected denning site to give birth, and enough land to keep them out of trouble with their deadly predator, humankind.

Other species can live only in very particular habitats. The giant saguaro cactus is found only in the Sonoran deserts of Arizona. It can survive temperatures that rise over 120°F, standing unprotected in the brutal sunlight for weeks without rain. It seems that if the saguaro can survive under such conditions it could take anything. But these impressive plants are found only in areas where the sparse rainfall comes during two periods—in the winter and late summer. Smaller cactuses can survive where it only rains during the winter. But the giant saguaro needs the extra summer moisture so it can bloom and set seed.

The saguaro requires other special conditions for survival, too. It cannot root in soft sand, for it will topple over if its shallow roots can't grab onto rocks of a certain size in the soil. If the rocks are too big, the roots cannot penetrate and spread adequately, so the rocks must be just the right size.

Observing Adaptations

Adaptations to a particular habitat are often quite obvious. The saguaro's lack of leaves and its pleated stem that expands when filled with water and becomes more deeply pleated during drought are just two obvious signs that this plant lives in an arid environment. Other adaptations are less obvious. Most plants take in carbon dioxide through pores in their leaves during the daytime and combine it with water to produce sugars, using the energy of sunlight. Cactuses like the saguaro, however, keep their pores closed most of the day. They take in carbon dioxide during the cool of night and store it chemically until the sun's energy is again available for making sugars. In this way, they can avoid losing precious water through the pores in the heat of day.

You can tell a great deal about the preferred habitat of a plant or animal just by studying its physical appearance closely. Take birds' beaks for example. A seed-eating finch has a stout bill for cracking its hard

The giant saguaro cactus provides a home for many desert animals, such as birds that carve out nesting cavities in its thick stems.

The beak of the black skimmer is adapted for skimming food from the water's surface, while the pileated woodpecker's beak can hammer holes in tree trunks.

food, while a nectar-sipping hummingbird has an elongated, slender beak for reaching into long, narrow flowers. Swimming animals like ducks and bullfrogs have webbing between their toes to give them power as they swim. Perching birds have no webbing. Instead, they have narrow, flexible toes for gripping branches, while tree frogs have expanded pads on the tips of their toes for hanging onto leaves. Trees with abundant soft, broad leaves live where rain is plentiful, while evergreens, with their thick tough needles, can survive where rain is scarce.

Becoming Alike

The environment can be very powerful in shaping living things for survival. Plants and animals found in similar environments may resemble one another closely in key traits, even though they are not closely related to one another. The cactuses of North America look remarkably similar to plants from completely different families that inhabit deserts in other parts of the world. Like cactuses, these plants have developed leafless spiny stems. Some species resemble the saguaro, with pleated stems, while others look like the familiar prickly pear, with rounded pads. The desert environment is so demanding that it imposes similar solutions to the problem of survival on unrelated organisms.

Water is another strong selector of form. The bodies of sharks, tuna fish, and dolphins are similarly shaped, even though these animals evolved completely separately from one another. Lists of similarities among animals adapted to particular habitats could go on and on. These adaptations, these various solutions to the problems of survival in different environments, constitute a large part of the biodiversity of our planet.

Varieties of Life

In addition to the great variations that can be seen in familiar species that have adapted to different environments—the tough, bumpy skin

LEFT: Magnolia trees live in the humid South and have broad leaves.
RIGHT: Evergreens such as pines make up western forests, where
moisture is scarce.

of the land-dwelling toad and the smooth, thin, slippery skin of the
pond-living bullfrog, for example—there are the larger differences
that separate the living world into a number of very different groups.

My brother and I loved to play "Twenty Questions" when we were
growing up. One person would think up an object, and the others
could ask just twenty 'yes' or 'no' questions to figure out what the item
was. A key piece of information was whether the object was animal,
vegetable, or mineral. If something was alive or derived from living
matter, it was considered either animal or vegetable—those were the
living kingdoms. Now we know that life is not that simple.

Animal (okapi), vegetable (horsetails), or mineral (snow)?

The amanita mushroom is very poisonous.

Scientists today do not agree on just how many living kingdoms there are, for nature is rarely neat in how it operates. A common and widely accepted scheme describes five kingdoms. The microscopic bacteria and blue-green algae form one kingdom, called the Monera. Their cell structure is much simpler than that of other living things. Fungi, such as mushrooms, yeast, and molds form another kingdom. The familiar green plants have their own kingdom, as do the animals. The fifth kingdom, however, is still a hodgepodge collection of miscellaneous organisms like protozoans, brown algae, and red algae that don't fit in anywhere else. Sorting out their relationships is difficult. For the sake of convenience, many scientists lump them all together, creating the fifth kingdom. Others, however, prefer to split them into multiple kingdoms to emphasize their differences.

Each of these kingdoms is dazzling in its variety, much of which is unfamiliar to most people. The animal kingdom is commonly divided into thirty-two smaller groups called phyla (singular: phylum) that differ greatly from one another. Most people are familiar with members of the Phylum Arthopoda, which includes insects and crabs, and the Phylum Chordata, which contains animals with backbones like you, me, dogs, and elephants. But few people have seen representatives of many phyla such as the strange, parasitic Mesozoa, or the Placozoa, the most primitive and simple of all animals. In 1995, a completely new organism that lives on the mouths of Norwegian lobsters was described. This strange, tiny creature appears to represent a totally new phylum, bringing the total up to thirty-three.

The soil swarms with minute nematode worms, and the seas are home to a floating menagerie of tiny life forms such as diatoms, single-celled algae, and the larvae of countless species of marine animals. Most of the life on Earth remains an unexplored mystery to all but the most dedicated scientists. Even for them, the majority of living things remain undescribed or even undiscovered.

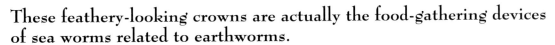

These feathery-looking crowns are actually the food-gathering devices of sea worms related to earthworms.

The yucca depends on the yucca moth for reproduction.

CHAPTER THREE
Links and Relationships

As a child, I was fascinated by the relationships among living things. I loved reading about the yucca moth and the yucca plant, how neither one could survive without the other. The yucca provides the moth's caterpillar with food and a home, and the adult moth in turn pollinates the yucca's flowers so it can make seeds and reproduce itself. It all seemed like such a tidy arrangement.

Later on, I came to realize that life is not that simple. The yucca and the moth certainly do depend on each other completely—if either one were to die out, the other would soon follow. But both require the proper habitat to survive. They need the right sort of conditions—a hot, dry place to live. If humans cover over too much of the desert with houses, roads, and shopping malls, there will be no place left for the yucca to take root and grow. Or if the climate on Earth changes, altering the rainfall pattern where the yucca lives, it could disappear, its roots rotting from too much moisture or shriveling up from too little rain.

Nature's Connectedness

Nowadays, we frequently hear the phrase, "Everything is connected." The principle of connectedness is especially true of biological systems. Perhaps the most basic form of connection is who eats whom. Grass grows in a meadow, fueled by sunlight, rainfall, and the minerals within the soil. Grasshoppers eat the grass, spiders feed on the grasshoppers, birds such as warblers consume the spiders, and hawks prey on the warblers. Since nothing feeds on the hawk until it dies and its body is decomposed by bacteria, fungi, and worms, it is the last link in its food chain. But each food chain is really not a chain at all—it is a web, with each species connected to a number of others by feeding relationships. Grasshoppers aren't the only ones to eat the grass—mammals such as deer consume it as well. The deer in turn are preyed on by predators such as mountain lions and wolves. And deer feed on more than just grass—they actually prefer to eat the tender young sprouts of trees and bushes when they are available. The grasshoppers, too, are eaten by a great variety of animals besides spiders—foxes and meadowlarks, for example. And the dead bodies of predators like hawks are not the only food for decomposers. Decomposers also break

Meadow spiders catch grasshoppers in their webs.

down dead grass, animal feces, and other remains of life into their chemical components.

If one species of grass should disappear from the meadow, all is not lost. Any insect that can feed only on that kind of grass would perish. But other grasses would replace the absent one, and the deer and grasshoppers would simply shift their feeding. The meadow would adapt, although its diversity would be diminished.

In their book *Extinction* Paul and Anne Erlich compare the progressive extinction of species on Earth with the gradual dismantling of an airplane. One by one, workers remove the rivets that hold the plane together. A potential passenger complains, concerned that the airplane might fall apart in flight. But the ground crew removing the rivets tries to reassure him—this rivet isn't essential and neither is that one over there, so there is nothing to worry about. The traveler, however, continues to worry. He knows that if too many rivets are removed, the

LEFT: A rough-legged hawk feeds on its prey. RIGHT: Deer are well camouflaged at the edge of the forest.

Purple sea urchins, seen here behind the green sea anemone, are a favorite food for sea otters.

A female alligator guards her nest.

plane and its passengers will be doomed. Like him, with his concern about those "nonessential" rivets, we should be concerned about the removal of species from our planet. It may seem that this species or that one is not essential—but who is to know what combination of extinctions could lead to disastrous consequences? Unlike that passenger, we cannot choose not to take the flight—we are all passengers on spaceship Earth.

Keystone Species

The consequences of loss of some species may not be obvious. But where others disappear, however, the results can be devastating. Sea otters once lived in protected kelp beds up and down the Pacific Coast of North America all the way from southern California to Alaska. During the nineteenth century, this appealing animal was hunted to extinction over most of its range, resulting in devastation of the entire kelp bed ecosystem. Sea urchins—spiny creatures that feed on kelp and other algae—are the primary prey of sea otters. As the otters disappeared, the urchins multiplied, consuming more and more kelp as their populations exploded. As the kelp disappeared, so did the multitude of life that depends on it, from tiny algae and corals that anchor themselves on the kelp to tiny snails that eat the algae and to the fish that find refuge midst the gently waving fronds. Fortunately, the otters survived in the north and were reintroduced into their old habitats. They reproduced quickly, feeding on the abundant urchins. As the urchin populations came under control, the kelp was able to repopulate its former range as well, followed by the rest of the ecosystem. Today, where the otters have been restored, the kelp forest has returned.

Species like the sea otter, whose presence supports so much life, are called "keystone species." The American alligator is another example. The alligator was intensively hunted for its fine leather and its delicately flavored meat until it had disappeared from all but the most isolated swamps and marshes. As the alligator disappeared, so did other animal life—fish, frogs, and birds alike. Why did this happen? The alligator feeds on these animals, so it would seem there should be more of them, not fewer, with the alligators gone. But during the dry season, alligators dig out ponds called gator holes. As the rest of the swamp dries up, animals that depend on water for survival move into the gator holes. No matter that the alligator consumes some of these creatures for food—the rest survive until the rain returns. When the alligators were no longer there to keep the gator holes open, the ponds filled with silt and plant life until the other animals had no refuge, so they disappeared as well.

When the American alligator was declared an endangered species and protected from hunting, it repopulated much of its old range within a few years. With its return, and the reappearance of the dry season refuges it provides for other animals, the variety of southern swamp life is coming back.

Unfortunately, keystone species are usually not obvious until they become scarce or disappear. Then the essential services they provide for ecosystems become evident when other species that depend on them start to have problems. Keystone species are only the most striking examples of how important living things are to one another, of how interconnected the living world is.

Homebodies and Wanderers

Once a seed has sprouted and become anchored in the ground, the plant has to deal with whatever comes its way—weather; other plants that compete for water, space, and sunlight; and animals that might feed on it. Most animals have the luxury of mobility—they can escape from the blazing sun or freezing cold by hiding in the shade of a plant or digging into the ground. They can also move about in search of food.

Creatures such as butterflies, bats, and birds have even greater freedom, the freedom of flight. They can move much more readily from

Land plants are anchored to the ground and must be able to take whatever their surroundings give them.

place to place than their earthbound relatives, and many take advantage of their mobility to escape climatic extremes. Northern-breeding birds that rely on insects for food have no choice—when winter comes, they must head for milder climates to find their prey. Other birds, like ospreys that feed on fish, also join the migration—their food is hidden during winter under the ice. An osprey that nests during the summer on a refuge in Massachusetts may spend the winter in a national park in Cuba.

This freedom to travel has served birds well until recently. As humans have taken over more and more of the natural world, migrating birds have faced new obstacles. Stopovers along the way, which the birds rely on for refueling, have given way to subdivisions and shopping malls. Dams have dried up rivers that produced fish and insects that the birds feed on. And when they reach their southern destina-

Birds, such as this osprey, can escape local climatic conditions by flying elsewhere.

tions, the birds often find that instead of forests, they are faced with a burned-over landscape on its way to becoming a cattle pasture.

From the 1940s to the 1980s, the populations of American songbirds dropped drastically. Once-common species are now rare, and birds have completely stopped returning to some areas where they once sang their beautiful songs, flashed their bright colors, and nested to produce more of their own kind. A major cause of this disappearance is the destruction of habitat both in their winter homes and along their migration routes. Migratory birds are especially vulnerable links in the connectedness of life, for their survival depends on healthy habitats scattered over thousands of miles of the Earth's surface.

Cedar waxwings winter as far south as Panama and the West Indies.

Tropical rain forests are being cut down at an alarming rate, destroying habitat for all living things. *Photo by Dan Perlman*

Changing Habitats

At first, scientists blamed the destruction of tropical forests for the decline in American songbirds. If only we could help preserve those distant stands of trees we could save our wandering birds. But then the scientists literally began to look into their own back yards, and they were not happy with what they found.

Tropical rain forests are not the only ones that are disappearing at an alarming rate—so are our own remaining woodlands. Especially in heavily populated regions, the woods are being reduced to smaller and smaller islands of trees. The consequences of the breaking up of our forests into isolated patches are grave.

Many songbirds nest in the forest interior. When they are forced to build their nests too close to the forest's edge, cowbirds defeat the songbirds' attempts to raise families. Cowbirds live in the open meadowlands and along the edges of forests. Rather than make their own nests, they are parasites on other birds. When an adult songbird is away from its nest, a female cowbird lays an egg there. Most songbirds are not aware of the alien egg and incubate it right along with their own. The cowbird's egg hatches rapidly into a large, aggressive chick that outgrows its nestmates.

The adult songbirds are unable to recognize that the remaining chick isn't their own and continue to feed it. Their own chicks can't compete and slowly starve. As a result, the songbirds raise a single cowbird chick instead of several of their own kind. As the forest patches become smaller and smaller, more and more songbirds are forced to nest close to the woodland edges and become victims of the cowbirds' deception. Fewer and fewer are successful at reproduction. Even if we can stop the destruction of the tropical forests, our own songbirds won't survive unless we can restore our own forests.

The speckled egg of a cowbird lies nestled with the eggs of a red-winged blackbird.

Many scientists believe life began in the ocean billions of years ago.

CHAPTER FOUR

The Origins of Diversity

How did the amazing diversity of life come about? The process began at the beginning, with the origin of life on Earth, and has continued through billions of years as living things changed through time.

No one can know for certain just how life on Earth began. Scientists have conducted many experiments in attempts to understand the processes involved. These experiments give us ideas about how life could have begun, but we cannot be sure of how it actually did occur.

We can be quite confident, however, of what began to happen soon after life came into existence. A key characteristic of living things is that they pass on their physical traits to their offspring. We can see this easily within our own families—you may have a nose like your mother's and hair like your father's.

The Importance of Natural Selection

A single concept, called "natural selection," is the key to understanding how life on Earth evolved over billions of years. In any population of a particular species, there are variations in the traits of the individuals, just as we see in human families. Natural selection means that an organism with traits that adapt it well to its environment is more likely to survive long enough to reproduce than an organism with less well-adapted traits. The adapted individual will therefore be more likely to have offspring. If the desirable traits are hereditary, they can be passed on to the offspring. In the next generation, more individuals will have the better-adapted traits. As the generations roll by, there will be more and more individuals that are better and better adapted to their environment. Natural selection was recognized and described by Charles Darwin in his book *The Origin of Species,* which was published in 1859. Despite all the advances in the study of genetics and evolution since Darwin's time that have uncovered other influences, natural selection is still seen as the most important force driving evolution.

A variation of natural selection, also described by Darwin, is called "sexual selection." In sexual selection, traits that make an individual more attractive to the opposite sex enhance its chances of reproducing and passing those traits on. The trait in question—brightly colored feathers in a male bird, for example—might not help it survive from

The Malaysian walking leaf is well adapted to its environment.

day to day. But if the trait makes the bird more attractive to potential mates, its likelihood of being passed on is increased. The same is true for traits such as the spurs on the legs of roosters that help an individual triumph over rivals.

Understanding Heredity

The science of genetics was not part of established science in Darwin's time, so Darwin didn't know how physical traits were passed from parent to offspring. Now we know that the information necessary to produce an organism is carried from one generation to the next as a simple code that is virtually identical throughout the living world. The code for physical traits is carried by the chemical DNA (deoxyribonucleic acid) which is contained within microscopic cell structures called chromosomes. DNA occurs in long, coiled strands. The DNA strands consist of a series of sections that code for characteristics such as hair color. The piece of DNA that controls a particular trait is called a "gene." It takes tens of thousands of genes to describe all the traits that make up one individual—about 100,000 genes for a human, for example. Each gene can exist in a number of forms, called alleles. The alleles code for variations in the trait the gene controls. In a skin color gene, for example, one allele might code for production of lots of the dark pigment melanin, while another results in only a small amount of melanin. An individual who carried the first allele would have dark skin while one carrying the second allele would be pale.

Every cell in the body carries basically identical copies of chromosomes within the controlling center, called the nucleus, of the cell. Each time a cell divides, it makes copies of the chromosomes so that each new cell has the same set of genes. The array of genes carried by the chromosomes in our bodies is the same in each cell, but our assortment of genes is different from our sisters or brothers. The same is true in most other species—each individual is genetically unique. There are a few exceptions to this rule, such as identical twins, but these exceptions do not affect the fundamental processes of evolution.

The chromosomes exist as pairs in most organisms. One chromosome in the pair came from the female parent while the other came from the male parent. Thus, each individual is different from its parents—it gets only half its genetic material from each.

Random Variations

Before an organism reproduces, the cells that yield the eggs or sperm divide in a different way than body cells normally do. Instead of dividing to produce two identical cells, each with a pair of each type of chromosome, the sex cells divide to produce four cells, each with one chromosome of each type. At the beginning of this special form of cell division, the two chromosomes of a pair come together and exchange parts. This process is called "crossing over." Crossing over, combined with the random distribution of chromosomes from the male and female parents, results in the differences among offspring from the same parents.

The Origin of Differences

The variations among organisms are the result of differences in the alleles of their genes. But how do the variations among the alleles themselves come into being? The process by which DNA makes copies of itself is very accurate. But it isn't always perfect. Sometimes mistakes, called mutations, are made. Mutations occur naturally at a low rate. Environmental factors, such as radiation or chemicals such as dioxin, can increase the rate of mutation. The mutations can result in changes in the trait carried by the gene. Some changes are so drastic they result in death. But others lead to the variations in traits that allow individuals to function better in their environments and, over time, for species to evolve.

All sorts of changes can result from mutations. Some of the most important ones can't be seen. For example, a mutation might alter the

One of these horses carries a gene that gives it a white marking on its face, while the other doesn't.

Each zebra has a different pattern of stripes.

structure of a cell chemical so that it operates better at a higher temperature than before. If the organism carrying the mutation lives in a warm climate, the change could help it survive, so the new allele created by the mutation would likely be passed on to new generations. If the organism lived in a cool place, however, it could be less likely to survive and might die before it reproduced.

Mutations can also result in differences obvious to the eye. The individual carrying the new allele might have a curly coat of fur instead of straight hair, for example. In some environments, the curly coat could be a good thing, while in others, it might create a disadvantage.

Evolution acts on the entire collection of traits of an organism. Some of those traits may be advantageous, while others are not. Chance always plays its part as well—a well-adapted individual could die before

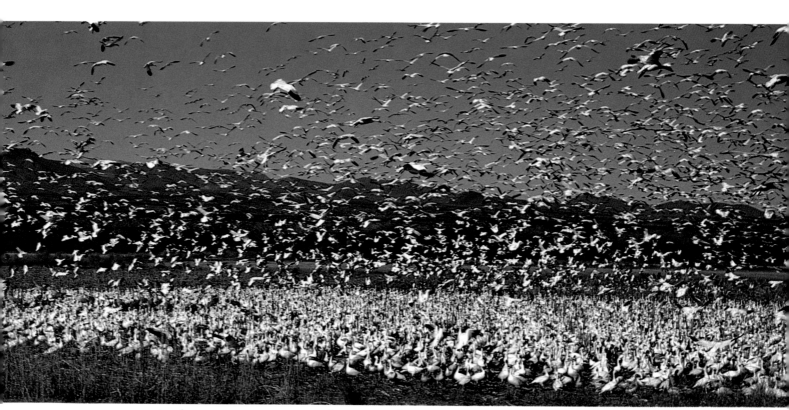

Evolution acts on populations of organisms, such as this flock of snow geese, not on individuals.

The endangered Antioch Dunes evening primrose lives in a very small area of sand dunes isolated through time from similar habitats in other parts of California.

it reproduces. Evolution ultimately acts on populations of organisms, not on individuals. The process is a matter of chance and likelihood. Generation after generation, the better-adapted individuals will have a better chance of reproducing and passing their traits to the next generation than the less-adapted ones. Over hundreds to thousands of generations, the result of this natural selection is evolution.

Species and Changes

As environments change, species must evolve to meet the new challenges presented to them or die out. Various forces, from the separation and drifting of continents to more local changes such as the shifting course of a river, can isolate groups of individuals of the same species from one another. When two groups, or populations, of a species are separated, they do not breed with each other and exchange genes. Over many generations, evolution will act on the populations, favoring different traits in each. Eventually, they may become so different that they can no longer breed with each other. They have become separate species.

It is very difficult for us to think in evolutionary terms, for evolution usually takes place over extremely long time spans. Humans usually think in terms of our own time scale, limited by a life span of around seventy-five years. Evolution usually works over spans of thousands to millions of years.

Extinction Is Forever

Almost everyone is fascinated by dinosaurs. The more we learn about them, the more amazed we become that such varied and vital creatures could disappear from the face of the Earth. How could it have happened? How could animals that survived for millions of years and filled so many different roles in nature have all become extinct?

By far the most common cause of extinction is very simple—a change in the environment makes it impossible for a particular species to produce enough offspring over time to replace the individuals that die. Extinction is usually a gradual process. As time goes on, the populations of the species become smaller and smaller until there are no more; the species is gone forever.

Any number of environmental changes can bring about extinction. The climate may change. Climatic changes can bring about extinction in a number of ways. The species itself may not be able to survive and reproduce under the new conditions. For example, some scientists believe one cause of the extinction of the thousands of different dinosaur species was lowering of the temperature of the Earth's atmosphere brought about by the crashing of a gigantic meteor. They believe that the impact sent enormous amounts of dust into the atmosphere, blocking sunlight and the warmth that comes with it. Most dinosaurs were probably cold-blooded, meaning their body temperature varied with the temperature of the air, like modern reptiles. Cold-blooded animals cannot survive in very cold climates because their bodies can't get warm enough for them to move about and find food.

Some dinosaurs may have been warm-blooded, meaning they were

Some glaciers in Alaska are receding, uncovering habitat that is quickly colonized by arctic plants. *Photo by Dorothy H. Patent*

able to keep their bodies warm even if the atmosphere was cold. Why, then, would these species have also died out? Remember that living things depend on other living things for their survival. If the food organisms that a particular species depends on become extinct, the dependent species won't be far behind, unless it can adapt to another source of food. Drastic changes in the environment can lead to cascad-

"Cold-blooded" animals such as salamanders can't survive in the far north.

ing extinctions—first some species die out, then the species that depended on them, followed by the species that depended on the second group, and so forth.

Five times during the last half billion years, mass extinctions killing off the majority of species on Earth have occurred. While we do not know the reasons for these great losses of biodiversity, we do know that they were caused by forces of nature. There is nothing we can do about natural changes in the environment that lead to extinctions. But we can hope to become aware of how human activities can bring about the oblivion of extinction and do what we can to avoid such losses.

As conscious beings, we have a responsibility to our home planet to care for it and do our best to keep it a healthy place for all liv-

Golf courses eliminate large areas of natural habitat, while at the same time creating new habitat for other animals, such as Canada geese.

ing things. Our health is linked to the Earth's well-being. We breathe the air and drink the water, and we eat plants grown in the soil and animals that feed on those plants. What affects other life affects us as well.

If we continue to poison and destroy the Earth, we can bring about our own wave of mass extinction, which might include the elimination of our own species. But even if humans were to survive such a catastrophe, our emotional and spiritual lives would be severely diminished. If some life survived, it could evolve once more into a diverse array. But evolution on the large scale occurs over tens of thousands to millions of years. None of us would be around to appreciate the next explosion of diversity—if it were to occur.

Crop plants such as corn feed us and our animals, but growing them
destroys large areas of natural habitat.

CHAPTER FIVE

Humans and Nature

Throughout human history, people have changed their environment to make it more suitable for human life. This ability to alter our environment, to create habitats in which we can thrive, is the secret of our success as a species. We can stitch clothing and build houses that protect us from the extremes of climate. We produce weapons that make us masters of the hunt. We grow foods that feed us well, and we raise domesticated animals that provide us with meat. As a result, humans are the only species to inhabit every continent on Earth, including Antarctica.

But our ability to alter the environment comes at a price to the planet. Every time people have colonized a new region, they have brought about the extinction of large numbers of native species. Our destructiveness to the environment is not a new habit—it has always been with us. It's just that in modern times, we have become especially effective at devastation.

In the Wake of Man

Evidence is strong that when people settle a new land, they drive many species into extinction. Humans (Polynesians from the north, called Maoris) arrived in New Zealand about a thousand years ago. At that time, about thirteen different species of flightless birds called moas made New Zealand their home. The smallest was turkey-sized, while the largest was a giant weighing at least 500 pounds (230 kg). These birds were especially interesting from an evolutionary point of view, since they occupied the ecological niches filled in other places by medium-sized to large mammals. There were no mammals in New Zealand, so the birds evolved to fill their roles.

When the Maori people arrived, they feasted on the moas. The birds were easy prey. They could not fly, and they had evolved in the absence of powerful predators such as humans. Within a few hundred years, the Maoris extinguished what had taken evolution millions of years to produce. There were many other victims as well. Twenty other land bird species, flightless insects, and a number of unique frogs also disappeared.

Hunting wasn't the only cause of these extinctions. The people cut down trees, destroying forest homes for animals, and they burned the land. Rats arrived with them and made fast work of the eggs of ground-nesting birds and small land animals.

The story is the same in other places. The Polynesian islands stretch through the southern Pacific Ocean from north of New Zealand across to the Hawaiian Islands, over 2,000 miles from the shore of North America. The larger islands are volcanic in origin and provide unique opportunities for evolution. These islands were conceived in fire and molten rock far from land. At first, they were devoid of life. Over time, wind and water gradually broke the rock into sand and pebbles, producing an environment in which plants could take root.

But life arrives at such places only by chance. Wind and weather bring random plant seeds, insects, and birds to the empty shores. Once there, some of these colonists become established. Over the millennia, unique species of insects, spiders, birds, other animals, and plants evolved on Polynesian islands and others far from land to fill the various ecological niches. Since most mammals lack the wings to make the long journey, they don't show up on oceanic islands far from continental shores, except for sea mammals such as seals. Island creatures are

Plants such as thistles, with seeds that move on the wind, can colonize islands.

Elephant seals breed on islands.

especially vulnerable to extinction when humans arrive, since they have no defenses against large predators.

The Polynesian people settled the islands like stepping stones, over a period of about three thousand years, starting at the western end with Fiji, Tonga, and Samoa, and arriving in Hawaii about 300 A.D. When they reached a new island, they found new species of birds, many of them flightless, all of them unused to being hunted. Since the islands often lacked good farmlands, the birds were the easiest food to obtain. When the people had killed off most or all of the endemic species—those found only in that place and nowhere else—some of them launched their canoes and headed eastward toward new tropical paradises.

The list of extinctions they left in their wake could go on and on—unique kinds of pigeons, starlings, doves, and many other kinds of birds. All through the islands lived different species of flightless rails. Each island had its own unique kinds, but today they survive only in New Zealand and on tiny Henderson Island.

The Hawaiian Islands were the last refuge for these seafaring people. The islands were also the largest of the Polynesian islands except New Zealand. Before people arrived, Hawaii was home to endemic birds such as an eagle much like the American Bald Eagle; several short-winged, long-legged owls; and a flightless ibis. Strange ducklike birds with huge legs, tiny wings, and powerful beaks appear to have filled the same ecological niche as the giant tortoises of the Galápagos Islands off the coast of South America. The Polynesian settlement of the Hawaiian Islands resulted in the extinction of as many as fifty-five such unique bird species.

When the Polynesians arrived they brought along some domesticated animals, including pigs. Over time some pigs became wild. The Polynesian pigs were small. Europeans later brought large pigs which bred with their smaller cousins to produce a destructive animal. These wild pigs uproot plants from the forest floor and have destroyed much endemic plant life. Some Hawaiian parklands are now being sur-

A bird similar to the bald eagle once lived in Hawaii.

rounded by fences to protect native plants, such as the silversword on Maui, from the pigs.

By the time Captain Cook arrived in 1778, all the big endemic birds had disappeared in Hawaii, but around fifty species of interesting small birds still survived. In the ensuing two centuries, a third of these have also become extinct. The coming of European settlers brought similar further losses of biodiversity to the other Polynesian Islands.

Large Mammals Disappear from America

Before humans arrived in North America after crossing the Bering Strait from Siberia, a fabulous variety of large mammals lived on the grassy plains. Wild horses—a different kind than lived in Eurasia—three kinds of mammoths, numerous antelope, camels, and a now-extinct bison species all shared the land. Unlike flightless Polynesian birds, these animals were hunted by powerful predators such as saber-toothed tigers and dire wolves. A wide assortment of scavenging birds thrived on the meat left on carcasses when the large mammals died, including now-extinct condors, storks, and eagles.

Even though they were being hunted by four-footed predators, the mammals were not ready for two-leggeds using weapons like powerful spears. While some scientists believe climatic changes brought about the extinction of many of these species, evidence is strong that humans were the cause here, as elsewhere. The disappearance follows the path of human settlement of the continent, and charred bones of the now-extinct species have been found with the charcoal of ancient cooking fires. If climatic change were the cause, why are the species of grasses, butterflies, and wildflowers the same today on the prairies as they were before human settlement? The disappearance of the mammals also brought about the extinction of many of the scavenging birds, for their main source of food disappeared along with the mammals.

ABOVE: The American bison did not become extinct when humans first came to America. European settlers, however, almost eliminated them during the 1800s.

BELOW: The same wildflowers grace the North American prairies as lived there thousands of years ago.

Humans and Extinction Today

Wherever humans settle, they bring with them destroyers of native wildlife and plants—the habit of hunting; domesticated animals such as goats, that consume native vegetation and trample birds' nests; rats, that eat eggs and insects; and deforestation and fire, which can destroy entire habitats.

Modern humans are even more destructive than their ancestors, however. Today, in addition to the continuation of all these classic causes of extinction, we produce massive quantities of poisonous chemicals. These chemicals pollute the land and water and destroy native species of plants and animals. For example, the pesticide DDT was once used all across America to control insect pests. Then fish-eating birds such as pelicans and bald eagles began to disappear. Fortunately, scientists were able to link the population crashes of these birds with

Power plants that provide us with electricity to make our lives comfortable bring with them pollution.

Brown pelicans, once endangered, have recovered through conservation efforts.

high levels of DDT that accumulated in the bodies of the fish they ate. When DDT entered the birds' bodies, it interfered with eggshell formation. The shells were so thin and fragile that they broke before the chicks could hatch. This discovery led to the banning of DDT in the United States. At first, no one knew if the bird populations could recover. But fortunately, with government attention and protection, birds like brown pelicans and bald eagles have been increasing in population, and the bald eagle is no longer considered endangered over most of the country.

We do not know what effects the many chemicals used in our industrial world may have on living things, including ourselves, but ominous evidence is developing. For example, scientists are very worried about the falling life expectancy of Russians. Between 1991 and 1994, the life expectancy for a Russian man fell from sixty-four years to fifty-seven years. Life expectancy for an American man in 1994 was seventy-two. Environmental abuse appears to be a strong factor in this alarming development. During the Communist years, factory workers and farmers

This pasture on Volcán Cacao in Costa Rica was once a lush rain forest.
Photo by Dan Perlman

were exposed to unregulated doses of pesticides and other hazardous chemicals. Nuclear weapons were openly tested, unsafe nuclear power plants were in operation, and toxic substances flowed into rivers. In addition to men dying young, deadly birth defects in Russia are more than four times as common as in the United States. Such problems take many years to develop, but once the effects are felt a great deal of damage has already been done and clean-up is very costly. While the United States and Canada have much better regulation of dangerous substances than did the Soviet Union, what is happening in Russia can serve as a warning not to brush off concerns about the cumulative effects of many potentially harmful chemicals in our air, soil, and water.

We also alter the environment in other ways undreamed of by early peoples, such as building giant dams that prevent salmon from swimming upstream to lay their eggs. Salmon that once swarmed through rivers in the Pacific Northwest are now almost extinct. We also build homes, highways, and shopping malls that destroy the habitats of species with limited ranges. Without homes, the species quietly die out.

The human population is exploding almost worldwide, putting pressure on natural environments to give way to the need for firewood, agricultural lands, and homesites. Human greed often gets in the way of long-range thinking. In developing nations, wealthy timber companies cut down the forests. In some countries, large ranches then take over the land to raise their cattle. When the land is exhausted, people move on, leaving behind a useless, ugly, degraded environment devoid of diversity. Here in North America, timber companies clear-cut our national forests, leaving a devastated landscape that cannot support the life that the forests once sheltered.

Human poverty in this overpopulated world is a major cause of endangered species. When a poor person in Africa or Asia can make as much money from one rhinoceros horn as he would earn in many years of hard labor, the temptation to hunt and kill illegally is very strong. We need to help the world's poor find ways to benefit economically from their environments without destroying them.

We need also to change the way we think about our place in the world and learn how to live in a sustainable fashion with nature. Ultimately, we depend on nature to sustain ourselves. Our food supply, our water, our air, our health, and much of our pleasure in life all begin with Earth and the diversity of life our planet supports.

We must preserve wildlands, especially those that harbor the greatest biodiversity. And when we do alter natural environments, we must do so in thoughtful ways that cause as little harm as possible to natural systems.

Plans to protect biodiversity must take local people, such as these Guatemalans, into account. *Photo by Dorothy H. Patent*

Here are just two of the varied moths that live at San Gerardo.
Photo by Dan Perlman

CHAPTER SIX

Studying Biodiversity

I'm lucky enough to be among the first visitors to the San Gerardo research station in the International Children's Rain Forest in Costa Rica. Night falls fast in the tropics, and the harsh fluorescent bulbs inside the unfinished building provide the only illumination by 7:00 P.M. The windows have been installed, but the doors have not, and moths are drawn from the blackness into the light. The rough wooden walls and the insides of the windows are soon dotted with their varied forms. I walk over to one window—a normal-sized one, about two feet by three feet. On just this one window I count twenty-five moths, each a different species. They range from a barely visible white one with folded wings to a three-inch beauty, its intricately patterned black and white wings spread flat. Looking closely, I see that despite their variety, they are all clothed in camouflage that would make each invisible on a different surface, most likely the bark of trees. One is orange-brown, like the wood used to build the station; another is a rich gray, which must match a different kind of forest tree. The diversity of the moths hints at a corresponding diversity of trees and, indeed, the rain forest is famous for the large number of tree species that can be found in just about any area scientists choose to study. I see just this small sample of diversity—I'm only looking at moths, and only the moths attracted to the lights in this one spot on this one evening—and I wonder. Moths, trees—and butterflies and beetles and ants and—how can this abundance ever be studied, cataloged, much less understood?

Costa Rica Plunges In

Costa Rica is one of the world's smallest countries, but it harbors one of the most impressive assortments of biodiversity in the world. The wild places of Costa Rica are home to a tremendous variety of living things—a greater variety per unit area than in almost any other place on Earth. Why is this so? What factors foster such an abundance of life forms?

Occupying a critical location in Central America, between North and South America, Costa Rica is home to species related to those of both continents. There are berries that would look at home in a northern forest living next to wild hibiscus flowers whose relatives thrive throughout South America. Scientists estimate that in the country's varied habitats, from the dry Pacific coast, across the high mountains (over 12,500 feet) of the Continental Divide and down to the steaming Atlantic lowlands, about a half million different species live, reproduce, and die in Costa Rica. Fortunately, this small country cares about its biological heritage, and about a quarter of the land is protected in forest preserves, parks, and reserves.

In 1989, the Costa Rican government decided to act on the need to learn about its abundant living treasures in a systematic way and set up INBio (the National Institute of Biodiversity) to study and catalog the country's biodiversity, to promote nondestructive uses of biodiversity, and to educate the country's people about the importance of their national biological heritage.

One of INBio's most important tasks is the National Biodiversity Inventory. People dubbed "parataxonomists" collect plants and animals and carry out the initial cataloging of the specimens before sending them on to INBio. Each sample is carefully labeled with the date, location, altitude, and collecting technique used. Parataxonomists are not university scientists, but rather local people who have received special training in taxonomy. Since they are part of the local population, they can educate their neighbors about the importance of wildlands and biodiversity to the country's welfare.

Wild hibiscus grows in Costa Rica. *Photo by Dorothy H. Patent*

An INBio worker shows American students one tray of golden beetles collected in Costa Rica. *Photo by Dan Perlman*

One INBio contract gives the pharmaceutical company Merck the opportunity to examine species from the tropical dry forest. During the dry season, most trees there are bare, but still provide a home for howler monkeys. *Photo by Dorothy H. Patent*

At the INBio headquarters near San José, the carefully preserved specimens are further cataloged. Samples that can't be identified by local scientists are sent to international experts. Each specimen is given a bar code tag that can be read by INBio's computer system.

Through partnerships with private industry and scientific and conservation organizations around the world, INBio is finding ways to computerize and network biodiversity information so it can be easily accessed and shared with scientists everywhere, not just in Costa Rica. The latest technology, including artificial intelligence techniques and satellite methods for collecting biological information, goes into this effort to study just this one small country's biological treasury.

Cataloging the U.S.A.

Another effort at collecting and organizing biodiversity information has been underway in the United States for more than twenty years. The Nature Conservancy, a private nonprofit organization, began its National Heritage Program efforts in South Carolina in 1974. Since then, the program has expanded to include all fifty states, the Navajo Nation, four provinces in Canada, and fourteen Caribbean and Latin American countries, including Costa Rica.

The Heritage Program focuses on identifying and helping preserve endangered species and habitats. The information it collects is publicly available and is used by governments at all levels as well as by land owners, scientists, and conservation organizations.

In 1994, the United States government set up the National Biological Service (NBS), a governmental organization that focuses largely on coordinating and sharing the information available about our country's biodiversity. Federal and state governmental agencies, universities

Pine Butte Preserve in Montana is one of The Nature Conservancy's better known preserves. *Photo by Dorothy H. Patent*

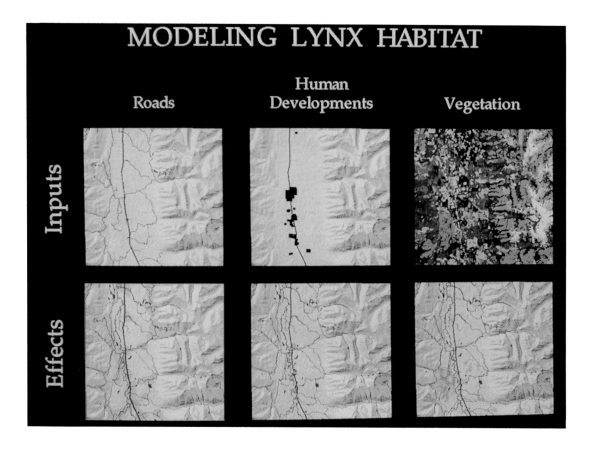

MODELING LYNX HABITAT

Roads | Human Developments | Vegetation

Inputs

Effects

around the country, and private groups like The Nature Conservancy all have a great deal of information about the plants and animals that live in the United States. An important goal of the NBS is to identify, organize, and integrate this data so that everyone has access to it by way of an electronic directory and network.

Technology and Biodiversity

Before modern computer systems, cataloging biodiversity would have been an impossible task. But thanks to technology, biodiversity information can quickly be retrieved, combined, and presented in a number of useful ways. In Costa Rica, for example, all an investigator needs to do to learn about a specimen is to scan its bar code tag with a light pen linked to the computer system. Within seconds, the monitor

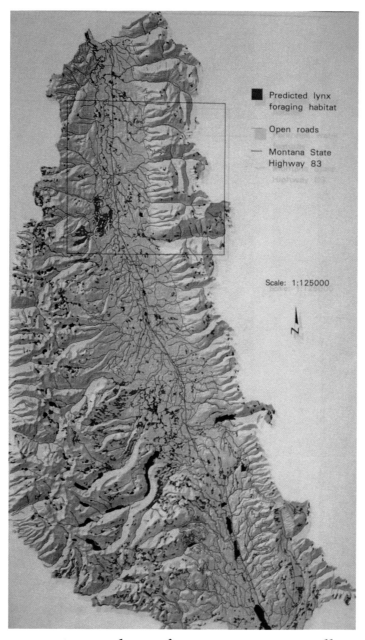

Predicted lynx
foraging habitat

Open roads

Montana State
Highway 83

Scale: 1:125000

N

LEFT AND ABOVE: Geographic Information Systems allow scientists to combine information from many sources onto one map. Here, roads, human developments, and vegetation were all combined on one map to predict habitat where the rare lynx might be found in and around the Swan Valley of Montana. *Courtesy of Roland Redmond, University of Montana*

When a satellite map showing vegetation features is draped over a contour map of the Swan Valley, using GIS technology, areas of clear-cut forest show up prominently in light green. *Courtesy of Roland Redmond, University of Montana*

screen displays information about the individual specimen and the species. The computer system can also sort information so the user can find out what other organisms were collected at the same time and place, what known range the species inhabits, and so forth. The computer systems of all the data centers involved with The Nature Conservancy's program (including INBio) can exchange information, so that a scientist in North Dakota can learn about a species or region in Costa Rica or any other area that is part of the system, and vice versa.

Geographic Information Systems (GIS) provide an especially powerful tool for biodiversity conservation. The kinds of maps we usually see show cities, counties, rivers, mountains, and roads. But all sorts of information can be displayed on a map. Maps can show the sites of nests of an endangered bird species, locations of particular habitat types, areas where the land is protected from development, and so forth. GIS technology makes it possible to superimpose different sorts of maps on one another using computers. This methodology can reveal important information. For example, when the locales of greatest biodiversity in Idaho were put on the same map with areas protected from development, scientists were alarmed to see that the most important areas in the state from a biodiversity standpoint did not correspond with protected areas. This information allowed them to focus their preservation efforts on the regions with the most biodiversity, to try to bring as much of that land as possible under protection.

Much of the Oroci Valley in Costa Rica has been turned into farmland. *Photo by Dorothy H. Patent*

CHAPTER SEVEN

Preserving Biodiversity

Around the world today, conservationists are looking for ways to save the world's remaining wild places. Their task is extremely difficult, for many reasons. The world economy doesn't favor conservation, it favors development, which normally means destroying the natural environment to build hotels, dams, factories, golf courses, and other sources of revenue. The developing countries in the southern hemisphere contain the greatest biodiversity on the planet, yet they also suffer from poverty and rapidly growing human populations. The poor of the world need places to live and ways to make a living. One of the quickest ways to meet these goals is to cut down forests to make room for farms. Ultimately, any plans for saving wildlands must take the local people into account. Otherwise, it is bound to fail.

Costa Rican Contradictions

I was shocked by what I saw when my husband and I got lost in the northwestern part of Costa Rica, near the border with Nicaragua. We were in one of the most environmentally conscious countries in the world, yet we were surrounded by the still-smoldering remains of what had been a beautiful rain forest. No birds sang, the air was silent. I could not bring myself to take photos; the images I held in my mind were painful enough. How could this have happened?

Costa Rica is a world leader in conservation efforts. Yet old laws designed to help the poor obtain land can encourage the legal destruction of the forests. The region where we were lost was slated for banana production. The poor people were clearing the land, which they would sell to international banana companies after gaining title. The companies would then own large tracts of former forest which they could turn into plantations. The poor would move on, some money in their pockets, to clear and claim the land of another forest. While about a quarter of Costa Rica's land is protected from development, the unprotected forests are being felled at a faster rate than anywhere else in the world.

Costa Rica is not alone in this problem. The economies and laws of modern nations have not been designed to foster conservation or to help the poor find ways of living on the land without destroying it. Until recently, conservation generally meant setting aside parks and other wild areas and keeping people out, except as tourists. People and

Once, a huge forest giant stood on this spot where only a stump remains. *Photo by Dan Perlman*

nature were viewed as incompatible. If wildness was to be preserved, it would have to be kept as free as possible from human influence.

In recent years, however, governments and conservation organizations have realized that people can coexist with nature—after all, they have done so for tens of thousands of years. The key is finding ways of using nature without destroying it. This concept—how to help people use nature for their own benefit without destroying it—is called "sustainable development." People must be integrated into the natural landscape and take sustenance from it so they have a stake in preserving natural diversity. Otherwise, biodiversity will continue to disappear as desperate people struggle to find ways to feed their families.

The Beginnings of Sustainable Development

Sustainable development can be carried out in a number of ways. The Children's Rain Forest is an international effort to preserve the forests

Native traditions teach how to live in harmony with nature. Here, a woman in Madagascar gathers medicinal plants.
Photo by Franz Minden Photos

surrounding the famous Monteverde Cloud Forest Preserve in the Costa Rican mountains. By 1994, children from around the world had raised money to help preserve 40,000 acres, and their efforts continue to expand. The Monteverde Conservation League, which manages the Children's Rain Forest, also has a tree nursery. Local farmers plant the trees as windbreaks which protect their fields. Fields with windbreaks produce better than those without them, and the rows of trees provide valuable habitat for birds and other animals. The League also helps educate children and other local people about the importance of the forest in their lives.

Rara Avis is a private rain forest preserve in Costa Rica dedicated to finding ways of using the rain forest without destroying it. Rara Avis

The Children's Rain Forest in Costa Rica preserves tens of thousands of acres of forest for future generations.
Photo by Dorothy H. Patent

has sponsored a butterfly farm, where tropical butterflies are raised for their pupae. The pupae are in demand by butterfly houses at zoos and gardens around the world, where visitors can walk midst tropical vegetation and watch beautiful butterflies from around the world up close. Rara Avis also plans to grow seedlings of the rare windowpane plant that is in great demand by florists and sell them. In addition, visitors to the Rara Avis preserve can sleep in the comfort of screened-in lodges and explore the unspoiled forests, guided by knowledgeable naturalists. The money spent by the tourists supports jobs for local people.

Preservation in the United States

The first step in any preservation effort is gaining the necessary knowledge, as we've seen with Costa Rica's INBio program and with our own National Biological Service. Partly through information gained during its Heritage Program inventories, The Nature Conservancy has designated regions of the country as "Last Great Places" bioreserves. In these areas, the Conservancy has purchased the land for core areas that will serve as reserves to protect the native flora and fauna. Around these core areas, the Conservancy is encouraging landowners to protect their lands from development. One powerful tool for protection is called a "conservation easement." A conservation easement means that the land can never be developed; it must remain in its natural state, even after the current owners die. Because the land cannot be developed, its value for taxation purposes does not increase as fast as that of developable land. Easements may also provide other tax advantages to the owners.

The Nature Conservancy and other preservation groups have helped protect much land in the United States. Recently, the Conservancy has applied the ideas of sustainable development to some of its American lands, including a cattle ranch in Wyoming that harbors the only known population of a rare plant called Barnaby's clover. In addition to protecting the plant, the Conservancy will use the ranch to

Logging with horses is much easier on the environment than using machines.

test methods for environmentally compatible ranching. A project in the Clinch River valley in Virginia, which is home to 136 rare and endangered species, involves logging with draft horses. Timber appropriate for use by local furniture and craft makers is selectively cut. By using horses instead of heavy machinery, damage to the forest and soil erosion are minimized.

Federal and state governments also protect wildlands in a variety of ways. Wilderness areas are free of any roads. Vehicles, including bicycles, are prohibited from trails, although horses are allowed. National parks are mostly protected from uses such as hunting, logging, and grazing. Wilderness areas can be enjoyed by hikers, campers, and hunters, while national parks are favorite destinations for many tourists.

National Wildlife Refuges were originally set aside to provide habitat for migrating ducks and geese. The money to buy and manage the

Wildlife refuges provide habitat for birds such as the yellow-headed blackbird as well as for ducks and geese.

Habitats for shorebirds such as the American avocet are protected by the Western Hemisphere Shorebird Reserve Network.

lands came largely from taxes on hunters. Today, the goals of the National Wildlife Refuge System are being redefined to take preserving biodiversity into account. Hunters, hikers, bird watchers, and photographers enjoy visiting wildlife refuges.

Other federal lands, such as our National Forests and Bureau of Land Management lands, are often managed with an emphasis on commercial benefits. The forests are logged, and many BLM lands are rented out to cattle and sheep ranchers at low prices for grazing. Many conservation groups believe these policies are harmful to the environment and are trying to get them changed to make them more environmentally sensitive.

International Efforts

The Convention on Biological Diversity negotiated in Rio de Janeiro in 1992 expresses the concern worldwide for the importance of conserving and utilizing biodiversity. Developing nations that are home to the greatest diversity of life want to be able both to preserve and benefit from that diversity. Once more, Costa Rica has been a pioneer in finding ways to gain economically from its biological riches while at the same time preserving them. INBio has signed contracts with pharmaceutical companies that allow the companies to look for medical uses of organisms living in Costa Rican parks. The companies pay for the privilege. Later on, if profitable uses are found, Costa Rica will receive a percentage of the profit from sales.

Countries around the world are also learning to cooperate with one another to help save species that cross international borders. The Western Hemisphere Shorebird Reserve Network coordinates reserves in the United States and a number of Latin American countries to protect migrating shore birds in their travels. As of September 1991, the seventeen preserves in the network protected four million acres of land and thirty million birds.

Where does Montana begin and Wyoming end, or vice versa?

CHAPTER EIGHT

Only One Earth

In 1968, the Apollo 8 astronauts snapped a striking photo of Earth from a new perspective. That image of a beautiful blue-and-white ball suspended in the blackness of space has helped change our vision of our planet. The image, which has appeared on posters and book dust jackets everywhere, shows without a doubt just how small and interdependent the Earth is. The thinness of our fragile atmosphere and the continuity of air, land, and sea are so strikingly illustrated that we cannot deny them.

The Illusion of Boundaries

When I learned at the age of eight that our family would drive across the country from Minnesota to California, I wondered what I would see when we reached the border of our state. How would I recognize it? But when we crossed the border from Minnesota into South Dakota, I saw no change whatsoever—the woods and farmland stretched out smoothly without interruption, not even a line of stone across the landscape. I realized then that there is no difference from one state to the next—such borders are imposed by people, not nature. State to state, country to country (even continent to continent in the case of Europe and Asia or North and South America)—borders are there to help people organize the world into definable units. They are not natural divisions.

But human boundaries can cause problems for living things. On one side of the United States–Canadian border, for example, wolves are protected; on the other side they can be shot. One country may value its wildlife and provide it with parks, while its neighbor may cut down trees right up to the border, eliminating habitat essential to the parks' inhabitants. Private lands can prevent wild animals from crossing from one protected area to another, and people may build homes in scarce winter habitat for grazing animals such as elk. Pollution is carried by rivers from one country to another, and chemicals emitted into the air from power plants in one country can silence life in the lakes and forests of its neighbors.

Sunshine Is the Source

Most of us live separately from nature. We cover our bodies with clothing. We get our food out of the refrigerator and from boxes and cans

The boundary through the wilderness between Canada and the United States is marked by a strip of bare land stretching for hundreds of miles.

This satellite map of the northwestern United States and southernmost Canada shows how borders are merely political boundaries. Habitat types, which show up in different colors, ignore the human divisions of the land. *Courtesy of Roland Redmond, University of Montana*

kept in the cupboard. Our houses and cars are heated during the winter and cooled in the summer, so our bodies are almost always at a comfortable temperature. We spend most of our lives indoors, surrounded by manmade objects and electronic gadgets.

We may live in an unnatural way, but we are still a part of nature, whether we are aware of it or not. We depend on the sunshine to provide the energy that produces all the necessities of life. Whatever the source of energy we use, it all can be traced back to the sun. Fossil fuels such as coal and oil are the remains of plants that lived on Earth in prehistoric times, taking the energy from the sun and using it to fuel their growth. The water that flows through dams to provide electricity was once part of oceans, lakes, and ponds. The water evaporated from the heat of the sun into the atmosphere, traveled with the air currents to higher altitudes, then fell as rain, joining the river above the dam.

The sun provides the energy that makes our food, too. All our crops depend on the sun's energy for growth, and domesticated animals such as cattle and pigs feed on plants that grow, thanks to the sun.

Freeways cut through the landscape carry us from place to place in air-conditioned cars, out of contact with nature.

Rivers and streams carry vital water from place to place.

Cotton thrives under the hot summer sun. Cotton provides us with both clothing and cottonseed oil used in foods, but growing it destroys natural habitat and often involves heavy pesticide use.

Our Living Bodies

Even though we cover them with clothing and feed them processed foods, our bodies follow the same biological rules as those of all other living things on our planet. Because of the unity of life on Earth, anything that affects one life form in a bad way is likely to do the same to other living things. We follow that principle when we test new food additives on bacteria or rats to see if they might cause cancer or other health problems. Such testing has pitfalls, however. DDT seemed harmless to warm-blooded animals at first, yet it almost wiped out birds such as bald eagles and brown pelicans. The safety tests that are carried out also do not take into consideration toxic effects of chemicals in combination and may also miss long-term problems.

Nature and the Human Spirit

Despite our habit of destroying the natural world without much thought, we have another side to our own nature—we appreciate and enjoy wild places and their inhabitants. We install bird feeders in our yards, we contribute money to save the rain forest, we visit the zoo to see "wild" animals, we go for hikes in the woods, and we take vacations in national parks and along the seashore. We like to poke around in tide pools and explore the wilderness. More people in the United States and Canada visit aquariums and zoos each year than attend all professional athletic events combined. In all, around 160 million Americans enjoy the outdoors as hikers, campers, bird watchers, and so forth. The industries that supply these hobbyists earn $18 billion each year manufacturing and selling the equipment people use in experiencing nature.

People may travel long distances to visit zoos and see animals such as tigers.

Glacier National Park is a popular tourist destination.

All these activities speak to our fundamental relationship with other living things as well as to the economic benefit of preserving nature. Spending time in natural environments can give us a feeling of peace many people can feel no place else, except perhaps in their place of worship. The presence of nature can help us sort out our thoughts and feelings and give us a perspective on our own lives.

If we destroy the natural world, assuming we could survive physically without the services it provides for us, what then? What sort of lives would we be bestowing upon our descendants? Because extinction is forever, no one can turn back the clock and bring back diversity that is lost. For ourselves and those that follow, we must do what we can to preserve the wondrous diversity of life on our beautiful planet.

Humans feel relationship to other species such as this orangutan.

Glossary

allele—a particular form of a gene—for example, a hair color gene might have different alleles for red, dark brown, blond, and black hair.

chromosomes—rod-shaped structures in the nucleus of the cell that carry the genes in a linear order.

cloud forest—a mountaintop forest which is almost always enveloped by clouds so that the surfaces of the plants are perpetually moist.

community—the populations of all species that occupy a particular habitat.

conservation biology—the study of biodiversity and how to preserve it.

crossing over—the exchange of DNA between the two chromosomes of a particular pair; crossing over occurs during the special cell division process that leads to egg and sperm formation.

DNA—deoxyribonucleic acid, the chemical that encodes the genes.

ecosystem—a community of organisms plus the physical environment in which it lives, including such factors as water, weather, soil composition, etc.

gene—the section of DNA that codes for a particular trait.

Geographic Information Systems (GIS)—computer methodology that allows different sorts of maps of the same area—one showing roads and one showing grizzly bear habitat, for example—to be superimposed on one another, providing valuable information for biological preservation work.

habitat—the environment within which a species is typically found, that meets its ecological needs.

Heritage Program, National—a systematic effort by The Nature Conservancy to catalog the biological inventory of the United States and some other countries.

INBio—the Costa Rican National Institute of Biodiversity, which catalogs and studies the country's biodiversity.

keystone species—a species that plays a crucial role in creating habitat for other living things; for example, alligators dig out small ponds, called gator holes, that allow many aquatic organisms, such as fish and frogs, to survive the dry season.

mutation—a mistake in the copying of a gene's DNA. Some mutations result in death or deformity, but a mutation can result in improved survival of an organism. Mutations result in the formation of new alleles.

mycorrhizae—soil fungi that make intimate contact with the roots of plants and provide the plants with important nutrients.

National Biological Service (NBS)—a governmental organization established in 1994 to coordinate and facilitate sharing of biodiversity information in the United States.

natural selection—the process by which individuals with adaptive gene combinations survive and reproduce, while individuals with nonadaptive gene combinations do not. Over time, natural selection leads to evolutionary changes.

parataxonomist—a person specially trained in the art of collecting, preparing, and identifying specimens from the field for biodiversity studies.

rain forest—a forest that receives at least four inches of precipitation each month of the year, most of the time. Rain forests generally receive considerably more rain than the minimum.

sexual selection—the increased mating opportunities of individuals possessing traits attractive to the opposite sex. Sexual selection is thought to be responsible for such spectacular features as the tail fan of the peacock.

The Nature Conservancy—a private organization devoted to preserving wild places, especially those containing rare or endangered species, or wide biodiversity.

Index

Page numbers in *italics* refer to illustrations.

About the Author and Photographer

Dorothy Hinshaw Patent holds a PhD. in zoology from the University of California at Berkeley. She has written more than eighty books for children and young adults on wildlife and wildlife management, most recently *American Alligator* and *Deer and Elk*. In 1987, Dr. Patent received the Eva L. Gordon Award for Children's Science Literature for the body of her work. She and her husband, Gregory Patent, have two grown sons. The Patents live in Missoula, Montana.

William Muñoz earned his B.A. degree in history from the University of Montana. He has collaborated with Dorothy Hinshaw Patent on many successful photo essays, including *American Alligator.* He lives with his wife, Sandy, and his son, Sean, in St. Ignatius, Montana, where he divides his time between freelance photography and skiing.